The Kid's Guide
to Grand Teton National Park

Written by
Charles Craighead

Photography by
Henry H. Holdsworth

**Official Guidebook
of Grand Teton National Park**

Published by
Grand Teton Association

Table *of* Contents

(GET THIS BOOK STAMPED) SEE PG. 54

A mule deer with her twin fawns.

WHAT is a national Park?

The United States was settled on the East Coast by our European ancestors. As the country grew and people moved West, they cut down forests, plowed the prairies, and cleared land for farms. They never thought about saving any of the land just as they found it.

By the time the first explorers reached the Tetons, many people believed that our country should save some of the beauti-

Kids grew up here before it was a park.

ful forests and open spaces. The animals should be protected or they would all be gone. In 1872, our country set aside the world's first national park. This was Yellowstone, not far from the Tetons. It was to be kept just as it was, so that everyone could visit and see how beautiful it was. It would belong to all of us.

Then the U.S. government created the National Park Service to watch over Yellowstone and other wild places. The forests would not be cut and the animals would not be hunted. Places that were important to our country's history were also saved.

Moose look small from far away.

A SPECIAL PLACE—
A SHORT HISTORY OF THE TETONS

Can you imagine what it would be like to live here thousand years ago? There were no roads, no stores, and no machines. The prehistoric Indians who lived on this continent had to find their own food, make their own clothes from animal skins, and build shelters made from wood and hides. They also had to live with animals that are now extinct—animals such as the giant ground sloth, the wooly mammoth, and the sabertooth tiger!

WASHAKIE

Chief Washakie was a great and wise leader of the Shoshone Indians. He had pure white hair. Washakie once adopted a twelve-year-old pioneer boy who ran away from home and took care of him for two years until he went back to his family. His name was Nick Wilson, and he later wrote a book about his adventures called The White Indian Boy. *He started the town of Wilson just south of the park.*

American Indians, homesteaders and ranchers liked this valley.

The prehistoric Indians left us signs that they had been here. They left arrowheads, spear points, and piles of stones where they made ovens and cooked food.

The American Indians were nomadic, which means that they did not build houses and towns as we do. They moved all around the West depending on the season. They traded things, learned new customs, and their languages and cultures grew.

The Shoshone Indians and other tribes still live near the Tetons, but of course they now live in towns and houses like everyone else. Like their ancestors, modern American Indians see themselves as a part of nature. Their history and culture is an important part of this park.

SHOSHONE WORDS

English	Shoshone
One	Semme
Two	Wahatehwe
Three	Bahaitee
Sun	Dabai
Moon	Muh
Water	Baa

AMERICAN INDIAN NAMES

American Indians in the 1880s had colorful and descriptive names. When he was born, Chief Joseph of the Nez Perce Indians was named Thunder Rolling in the Mountains. Many of Washakie's Shoshone people also had beautiful names. Some of them included these names:

HORSE'S GRANDFATHER

STAND AND LOOK

RABBIT CRYING

GRAB YOU AND THROW YOU DOWN

LOTS OF DOGS

RABBIT TAIL

Discovered Again— Trappers & Explorers

The first white people to come here were men who trapped animals for their fur. That was an important way of life back then, before there were any man-made materials like nylon or plastic.

The trappers explored the Rocky Mountains looking for beavers since their thick fur was very valuable for making hats. They were called mountain men because they lived in the mountains most of the time. The mountain men admired the Indians for their knowledge of the land and for their way of life. They learned the American Indian languages and traded with the different tribes.

The greatest skill of the fur trappers was that they could find their way through the mountains. They knew every river, every valley, and every lake. They learned to find their way with natural landmarks, like high mountains. One of their most important landmarks was the Teton Range. The three highest peaks—the South, Middle, and Grand Teton—could be seen for many miles. The Tetons had many names back then such as the Pilot Knobs or the Ghost Robbers. French trappers named them "les Trois Tetons," which means "the three breasts."

Mountain Men Names

Some of the fur trappers had nicknames they earned in the mountains or names they received from the American Indians:

Jim Bridger: Old Gabe

Thomas Fitzpatrick:
Broken Hand

Jim Bake:
The Redheaded Shoshone

John Johnson:
Liver-Eating Johnson

William Sublette:
Cut Face

Thomas Smith:
Pegleg

Jim Beckwourth:
Bloody Arm

Christopher Carson:
Kit Carson

Davey Jackson and Jackson Hole

Born in Virginia in 1788, David E. Jackson came west and was a fur trapper. Davey Jackson's favorite place to trap was right in this valley by the Tetons. It was named Jackson Hole for him in 1829. (A "hole" was an old trapper name for a valley.) Jackson Lake, Jackson Peak, and the town of Jackson are all named for him.

Menor's Ferry cabin and store on the banks of the Snake River

GRAND TETON

Mountain men had a rough life! Read this note that trapper Osborne Russell made in his journal on July 4, 1885, after capsizing his boat in the Snake River: *"I now began to reflect on the miserable condition of myself and those around me, without clothing or provisions or fire arms and drenched to the skin with the rain ... a group of human beings crouched round a fire which the rain was fast diminishing meditating on their deplorable conditions ..."*

Mount Moran, named for artist Thomas Moran.

EXPLORERS and SCIENTISTS

The first people that the mountain men guided here were scientists who mapped the land, gave new names to the mountains and lakes, and made lists of all the plants and animals they found. Some of them were geologists, people who study mountains and rocks, and they were fascinated with the Tetons.

The most important scientific expedition to explore the Tetons came in 1872. It was called the Hayden Survey. Their photographs of the Tetons and Yellowstone helped convince the government to start saving some of the land in the West.

First Ascent of the Grand?

We may never know for certain who was the first person to climb the Grand Teton. The prehistoric American Indians spent thousands of years near the mountains, and they left signs that they had climbed to other high places in the Tetons. Did one of them climb the Grand? We will never know.

In 1872, Nathaniel Langford and James Stevenson reported they had scrambled to the top, but they had no proof. It was customary for climbers to plant a flag or leave something for proof—they did neither of these.

On August 11, 1898, William Owen, Frank Spalding, Frank Petersen, and John Shive made the first proven ascent. Standing on each other's shoulders, dodging loose rocks, and climbing across steep ice and snow, the four men found a way up and finally walked side by side to the summit so they would all be "first" together.

William Owen led the first group to prove they had made it to the top of the Grand Teton. Mt. Owen, next to the Grand, is named for him.

HOMESTEADERS

George Greenwood cutting wood for winter

In 1884, two fur trappers decided to try to live here. No white people lived in Jackson Hole then. The two men brought everything on horseback that they needed to build log cabins and be farmers.

Gradually more and more people homesteaded in this beautiful valley. Soon, there were general stores and log houses and other buildings around Jenny Lake. Some of the people who lived here thought the buildings were ugly and ruined the view of the Tetons. They wanted to remove all the buildings and make the Tetons a national park. Other people wanted to build hotels, dam the lakes, or do whatever else they wanted.

This was a long fight. Eventually, the people who wanted a park won. In 1929, Grand Teton National Park opened. A very wealthy man named John D. Rockefeller, Jr. bought a lot of the land surrounding the park and gave it to the National Park Service. In 1950, his land was added to make the large park we have today.

Homestead house

Historic Places Today

Mormon Row   Want to know where people lived 100 years ago?

If you want to see where some of the farmers lived who homesteaded the valley, Mormon Row is the place. There are old barns, houses, corrals, and fences left from the early 1900s. This is a fun place to take photographs or make drawings. Most of the buildings are closed to preserve them, but you can peek into a few of them to see what they look like. This place was named Mormon Row because most of the pioneers who settled here were in the Mormon religion.

Menor's Ferry Historic District

If you only had one tiny store, what would it sell?

The first homesteader on the mountain side of the Snake River built these cabins. His name was Bill Menor, and he built a ferry to haul people back and forth across the river. In those days there were no bridges. Bill Menor had a store and a blacksmith shop, too. You can look in his old buildings and see how his ferry worked. There is a general store where you can buy the kinds of things that Menor used to sell.

Cunningham Cabin

Could you live in a house with only two small rooms?

If you think your room at home is small, imagine if you lived in this house with the rest of your family. This is the kind of home that the early settlers built and lived in. It belonged to a rancher and farmer named Pierce Cunningham. He was one of the first ranchers to think that it was a good idea to have a national park here.

Bison near homestead barn

Some people wanted to farm the land.

1929 - A NEW PARK

Early Jenny Lake rangers studying a map

The first park rangers climbed all the peaks, named the ones without names, and made rules for visiting the mountains. They also made trails and built campgrounds.

Other rangers studied the plants and animals and helped visitors learn about the new park. Jackson Hole and the Tetons were already famous for their wildlife, but now they were protected.

Facts & Figures about Grand Teton

Size: 310,000 acres, or 484 square miles

Highest Elevation: The Grand Teton, 13,770 feet above sea level

Average Elevation of Jackson Hole Valley: 6,800 feet above sea level

Height of the Grand above the Valley: 6,970 feet (1.3 miles!)

7 species of hoofed animals

22 species of rodents

17 species of carnivores (meat-eaters)

SCENERY AND GEOLOGY

How did these spectacular mountains get here? The Tetons almost look like they could have dropped out of the sky. In fact, it was just the opposite—the rock they are made of used to be deep in the Earth—but it didn't look like it does now. The process of making mountains like the Tetons takes millions of years.

The very outside of the Earth, where we live, is solid rock called the "crust." The solid center, or core, of the Earth is very hot, about 12,000 degrees. The outer part of the core is liquid rock. In between us and the core is the mantle, made of semi-solid rock that is like warm plastic or clay—it moves very, very slowly. As it moves, it breaks up the crust into huge pieces called plates, and they "float" on top of the warm mantle. North America is one plate, and there are others.

Up close and personal with rocks!

It's hard to imagine something the size of North America floating and moving, but it does—in super, super slow motion. When the plates push against each other, they fold up a little bit in the middle, just like when you push slowly on a blanket on top of your bed and it makes big wrinkles. When the plates stop pushing, they stretch back to where they were. This all takes millions and millions of years to happen.

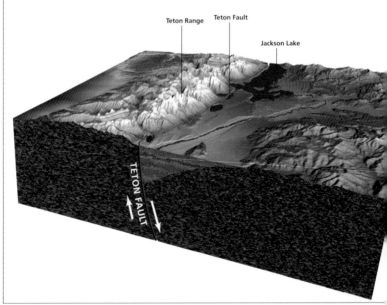

The Teton Fault created this scenery.

When the North American plate folded up, the Rocky Mountains formed. Then when it stretched back out, the planet's crust got pulled and pulled until it cracked. Those cracks are called faults, and they are found all over the world. One of them, the Teton Fault, happened right here.

After millions of years and many huge earthquakes, the two sides of the Teton Fault had moved over four miles—one side went up a mile and the other side went down three miles. It was like the sides of the fault were two big trapdoors lying on the Earth—one of them swung down and the other one swung up.

THE TETONS ARE STILL RISING AND THE VALLEY IS DROPPING

Humans live only a short time compared to the forces of geology, so we don't see things happening that take millions of years. But the Teton Fault that created the mountains is still there. The mountain side of the fault keeps rising, and the valley side keeps dropping—it just happens so slowly we can't see it or feel it. But geologists say that one day the fault will slip a lot at once, like it did in the past, and there will be a huge earthquake. No one can predict when.

THE TETON PEAKS

The side of the Teton Fault that rose up above the valley to become the Tetons is made of very old rock. It formed soon after the Earth began. This rock was deep in the crust, but it got pushed up because of the fault. As the rock of the Tetons got slowly lifted, it was just as slowly worn away by ice, water, and wind. Glaciers were the most important force that carved the Tetons into their shapes. All the rock that got worn off the Tetons and nearby mountains filled up the valley and made it level ground.

ALBRIGHT PEAK— 10,552 ft.
Named for Horace Albright who wanted this place to be a national park.

STATIC PEAK—11,303 ft.
Named for its frequent lightning strikes.

BUCK MOUNTAIN—11,938 ft
Named for mapmaker T.M. Bannon and his assistant George A. Buck who built a pile of rocks on top they named "Buck Station."

MT. WISTER—11,490 ft.
Named after Owen Wister,

author of *The Virginian* and an early visitor to Jackson Hole.

SOUTH TETON—12,514 ft. Named for its position south of The Grand.

MIDDLE TETON—12,804 ft. Named for its location among the other high peaks.

NEZ PERCE—11,901 ft. Named for the Nez Perce Indian tribe.

GRAND TETON—13,770 ft. Once named Mt. Hayden after explorer Ferdinand V. Hayden but the name didn't stick.

MT. OWEN—12,928 ft. Named for William Owen, first man to climb the Grand.

TEEWINOT MOUNTAIN— 12,325 ft. Named for Shoshone Indian word "Tee-Win-At" meaning "pinnacles." It's pronounced "tee-win-ott."

MT. ST. JOHN—11,430 ft. Named for Orestes H. St. John, a geologist with the 1872 Hayden Expedition.

MT. MORAN—12,605 ft. Named for landscape artist Thomas Moran.

View of the Tetons from Cunningham Cabin

GLaciers – ice on the Move!

GLACIER

TERMINAL MORAINE

Glaciers are still here!

The glaciers that carved the Tetons were part of an ancient time called the Ice Ages. A glacier is formed when snow builds up over time and turns to ice. This ice gets so heavy that it starts to get pulled down by gravity and "flows" slowly downhill.

The last of the big glaciers melted away about 14,000 years ago. They left many signs that they were here. One of the main signs left by a glacier is a big pile of rocks called a moraine.

Glaciers are so big and heavy that they can act like bulldozers and push everything out of their way. Glaciers only move as fast as an inch or so a day. They scoop up rocks and dirt, and anything that falls on them gets carried slowly along, too.

When the climate gets warmer, the glaciers stop flowing because no more ice is forming in the mountains, then they begin to melt. A melting glacier is said to be retreating. As the glacier

THE ice CUBE experiMent....

Purpose: *To see how ice can move.*

Materials: *A square cake pan, a brick or flat rock, a wire cooling rack, a freezer.*

The experiment: *Fill the cake pan with water and put it in the freezer overnight. Then take the ice out of the pan in one piece and put it on the wire rack in the freezer. Place the brick or rock on top of the ice. Leave the ice in*

melts, it leaves behind all the rocks and dirt it had pushed and carried. The biggest pile is at the front of the glacier, and it is called the terminal (end) moraine. Some glaciers also have lateral (side) moraines.

You can see many moraines in the park. They are low rocky hills covered with trees, usually circling a lake such as Jenny Lake. There are also big moraines in the middle of the valley. They are covered with trees and are not very high.

Twelve glaciers still exist in the Tetons. There was a Little Ice Age about 600 years ago when some small glaciers formed in the mountains. They can be seen from the Teton Park Road. Those small glaciers are still carving the mountains.

THE FIRST GEOLOGIST

Fritiof Fryxell (pronounced Frit-ee-off Frix-ell) was the first park geologist, in 1929. He loved the Tetons and all their different kinds of rock. He was also a good mountaineer, and he was the first to climb some of the peaks. He named many of them. Fritiof Fryxell wrote books about geology and about mountain climbing.

SEE HOW ICE CAN MOVE

the freezer for 24 hours, and then look at the bottom of it where it rests on the wire rack.

What happens: *The ice will start moving down between the wires of the rack. This is because the weight of the* brick pushes down on the ice and makes it softer on the bottom. Real glaciers do the same thing. Ice in a glacier starts to move downhill when it gets to be about sixty feet thick.

U-SHaPeD canYons & V-SHaPeD canYons

*If you look at Cascade Canyon from Jenny Lake, you might notice that it is slightly rounded and shaped like a big letter **U**. This is a sign that it was carved by glaciers. The ice was wide and thickest in the middle of the canyon, so it carved a rounded bottom with sides that are straight up and down.*

*If a canyon gets carved by a stream or river, the canyon ends up looking like a large letter **V**. This is because the stream is narrow, and it cuts straight down. The canyon doesn't get as wide, so the sides are angled steeply like a **V**.*

OTHeR GeoLoGY

Glaciers caused almost everything you see in Grand Teton National Park. The lakes were dug out by glaciers, and their moraines act like dams to help hold the water in. If you look at the lakes from a high point, such as Inspiration Point or Signal Mountain, you can see a tree-covered moraine around each lake. Even Jackson Lake, the largest lake in the park, was dug out by huge glaciers.

Rivers and streams in the park follow old channels made by water from melting glaciers. All of the streams that come out of

the mountain canyons also follow old channels made by melting glaciers. Today, melting snow and small glaciers are still the source of these streams. Most of these mountain streams empty into lakes at the bottom of the mountains, then they flow out and go to the Snake River. If you look at a map of the park, you can trace the path of water from high in the mountains all the way to the Snake River.

Some canyons are so deep that they go almost all the way through the Tetons. If you hike up one of them you will find a dead end where the glacier started. (This is called a cirque.) Look at Cascade Canyon and think of what it would look like filled to the top with ice.

Interesting Stuff: GEOLOGY and LIFE

Geology is a study of the forces that shaped this park, made the mountains and valleys, and formed the lakes. Geology also determines where plants grow, where animals live, and even where people live.

Look around at the park and notice where trees grow and don't grow. Why do you think forests grow on one side of a hill and not on the other? Look at the herds of bison. Why do you think they live where they do? And when you visit one of the historic sites, such as Mormon Row, ask yourself why the homesteaders decided to settle there.

If you can't think of any answers, you might ask one of the park naturalists.

Hint: Geology determines where topsoil forms, where the water flows, and where the sunshine can reach. This in turn determines where plants can grow, and animals either eat plants or other animals that eat plants!

Snake River

Male elk are called bulls.

AniMaLs & PLanTs

Grand Teton National Park is famous for its wildlife. There are some very large animals such as moose and bison, and there are small animals such as hummingbirds and mice. All of these animals are important in keeping the park's nature in balance and healthy. And just as important are all the plants. Without them, there would be no animals.

WiLDLiFe—anD THe PLaces THeY Live

If you look around the park you might notice that there are different groups of plants. There are forests, meadows, and fields of sagebrush among other groups. Biologists call these "natural communities" because they are a mix of wild plants and animals all living together and depending on each other, just like a community of people. (See the map in the back of the book for examples of community locations and their associated wildlife.)

ELK

Elk are in the Deer family, but are much bigger than regular deer. They are almost as big as moose but not as heavy. They are graceful animals. Elk usually spend days in the forest and come out into meadows in the evenings to feed. You will often see them in small herds of fifty or so animals. Elk are grazers, meaning that they eat mostly grass. The males, called bulls, have large antlers. The females, called cows, don't have antlers. Their calves are born in the spring. In the fall the bulls "bugle" their challenge to other bulls, and they often fight with their antlers. This is their mating season.

FUN FACT: Elk live to be about twelve to fifteen years old, but some may reach twenty. Elk migrate to places without much snow for the winter. Many of them go to the National Elk Refuge just outside the park.

MULE DEER

Mule deer have very large ears. In early summer their new coat is reddish brown, but it fades to gray by late autumn. The males shed their antlers in the winter and regrow them in the spring.

Mule deer migrate up into the hills in spring and back down in winter. They prefer to spend their days in forest and come out at dusk to feed in meadows.

Mule deer prefer mixed forests of aspen and pine and hillside meadows. Look for them on the park's moraines (the hills made by glaciers that surround lakes) and along trails into the canyons. Look in the aspen trees near Lupine Meadows, along the Leigh Lake Trail, and in the Signal Mountain area.

FUN FACT: Males are called bucks, females are does, and young are fawns. They live from five to ten years of age in the wild.

PRONGHORN

Delicate, deer-like animals with long legs, pronghorn have large heads with big eyes and blackish horns with prongs (points) on the front. The males have black markings on their heads and necks. Females have short horns without prongs. Pronghorn are commonly called antelope. The males are called bucks, the females are does, and young are fawns. Under ideal conditions, they may live ten years.

Pronghorns live in open grassland and sagebrush. Males are territorial and gather the females into bands. They prefer the grassland and sagebrush of Antelope Flats. Look for them in old hayfields from Kelly to Moose and near Lupine Meadows.

FUN FACT: Pronghorn are social animals, and in central Wyoming, they can form herds of 1,000 animals. Wyoming has the largest population of pronghorn in North America.

BISON

There is no mistaking bison—one of the largest mammals in North America. They are commonly called buffalo. They have huge heads, high shoulder humps, and short round black horns. The males are called bulls, the females are cows, and the young are calves. Both males and females have horns. Calves are a burnt orange color for the first few months.

Bison may seem tame, but they are unpredictable, and the bulls often charge without warning.

Bison live in the grasslands and meadows. In the park they are most common on Antelope Flats between Kelly and Moose. Bison may live to be fifteen to twenty in the wild.

FUN FACT: Bison are known for their "wallowing" behavior—rolling on the ground and making clouds of dust. This helps them groom their fur and soothe itchy skin.

COYOTE

Coyote

Gray wolf

Coyotes are medium-sized dog-like animals with pointy ears that usually point straight up and a furry tail with a black tip.

Coyotes are carnivores (meat eaters). They hunt mice and ground squirrels, scavenge large animals that have died, and eat insects and plants when they need to. They are usually most active at dusk and dawn. Coyotes form packs where there is plenty of food, but they are not as social as wolves.

Coyotes travel frequently in search of food. They can be seen just about anywhere in the park. Look for them in meadows and open areas in the sagebrush, along streams, and on the rolling hills in the eastern part of the park.

FUN FACT: The coyotes' natural intelligence and persistence make them popular characters in American Indian storytelling.

MOOSE

Moose are in the Deer family, and they are as big as a horse. They have long faces, large ears, and a beard called a dewlap. The males, called bulls, have big, wide antlers that look like an open hand. The females are called cows, and the babies are calves. Moose eat browse, which is the name for twigs and branches. They prefer to eat willows. Moose like to be near water and often wade or swim while they search for underwater plants to eat. Watch for moose in the willows, along the river, and near creeks and streams. They especially like beaver ponds.

FUN FACT: Sometimes a moose will hold its breath and go completely under water to find plants that grow on the bottom of a pond. The oldest known moose was age twenty-seven.

Black Bear

Although they are called black bears, they come in a variety of colors—cinnamon, black, brown, and blond. They have short claws and are excellent tree climbers. Black bears are most active at dusk and dawn. They usually live alone except for females with cubs. In their winter dens they do not hibernate deeply, but sleep soundly and awaken at times. Black bears feed on grass, berries, roots, insects, and carrion. In spring, they actively prey on young elk and deer.

Black bears prefer forests with lots of shrubs (especially berry bushes) and grass. Look for black bears in Death Canyon, Cascade Canyon, and in the forests around the lakes.

FUN FACT: Bears have extremely good memories, especially for food sources, which is why they should never get human food. A twenty-five-year-bear is old.

Grizzly Bear

You can tell grizzlies from black bears by their big shoulder humps and their fur that may have gray or white tips. They are most often a tan or light brown color. Grizzlies have longer claws than black bears.

Grizzlies feed on plants, mice, and ground squirrels. In early summer they prey on elk fawns, and at times grizzlies eat moths, pine nuts, gophers, or plant roots. Grizzlies hibernate in their dens from October or November until late March to early May.

FUN FACT: Since a grizzly's fur often has light-colored tips, which give it a "grizzled" look, oldtimers called the bears "silvertips." Grizzlies can live to age twenty-five in the wild and to forty or more in captivity.

Black bears can be brown!

Uinta Ground Squirrel

These little animals seem to be everywhere in the middle of summer. They are the only squirrel-sized gray animals you'll see in the valley, and they live in burrows in the ground. Look in the sage near park facilities and at scenic turnouts. They are common around the Menor's Ferry area, near Christian Pond, and along Mormon Row. They are often seen running around campgrounds, buildings, and picnic areas. Ground squirrels eat grass and other vegetation, but often "beg" for food from visitors. Please don't feed them—it is not good for them to eat human food.

FUN FACT: Uinta ground squirrels hibernate for six months of the year, so they spend most of their time eating to get fat for their sleep. Since they don't eat while they hibernate, ground squirrels need to live on their extra body fat.

CHIPMUNK

Chipmunks are easy to recognize by their small size and striped backs. There are several different kinds and sizes here, but they all look about the same. Chipmunks are members of the squirrel family and can climb trees and rocks easily. If it gets really cold and snowy, they hibernate for a while. Chipmunks that live near people get tame and beg for food. Please do not feed them.

FUN FACT: Chipmunks store piles of food for the winter and awaken from their deep sleep to eat.

GOLDEN-MANTLED GROUND SQUIRREL

You might see this little animal if you hike into one of the canyons in the Tetons. At first you might think it is a really big chipmunk, but if you look closely, you will see that it doesn't have any stripes on its head. These ground squirrels eat mostly grass, seeds, mushrooms, and berries, but they eat snacks that hikers drop or throw to them. This food is not good for them, so please don't feed them. Look for chipmunks along the park trails, especially in Cascade Canyon around Inspiration Point.

FUN FACT: The young are born about the first of June in litters of two to eight and are almost full grown in two months.

PORCUPINE

These large rodents with their stout, rounded bodies and quills are easy to identify. Porcupines are active all year, usually at night, and feed on tree bark, shoots, buds, and other vegetation. They den in caves and hollow logs.

Look for porcupines in the forests along the foot of the Tetons. One clue is whitish, freshly gnawed bark near the tops of pine and spruce trees. Porcupines do not throw their quills, but when the animals are frightened, their quills detach more easily. American Indians use dyed quills to make intricate, beautiful decorations on clothing and for certain jewelry.

FUN FACT: An average adult porcupine has about 30,000 quills on its body!

Pika

The only way to see this unusual little mammal is to hike into the mountains. They are often hard to find, even though you might hear them making their funny little "bleet" call. Look for them sitting on top of rocks along the canyon trails. Pikas look like tiny rabbits. They scurry around the rocks, cutting grass and flowers and piling them into a "haystack." This will be their food to eat through the long winter. Pikas don't hibernate. They live under the snow in caverns and tunnels.

A pika is about the same size as a guinea pig. It has round ears and no tail.

FUN FACT: Pikas have a second, smaller set of front teeth right behind their main ones.

Yellow-Bellied Marmot

These large, heavy-bodied rodents are familiar to hikers and climbers in the Tetons. Their fur is brown to yellowish, with an orange to yellowish belly, and a furry tail. Marmots live in colonies and have complex tunnel systems under the rocks. They hibernate eight months of the year from September to May! During the summer months they feed constantly on vegetation. They love to sun themselves on rocks. Marmots are most commonly seen along trails leading into the mountains.

FUN FACT: There is also a beautiful, jet-black variety in the Tetons. This is a "melanistic" color phase of the same species.

Yellow-bellied marmot

A baby crane is called a colt.

SanDHill CRane

The Sandhill Crane is a beautiful all-gray bird with a red cap on its head. It is about four feet tall with long, long legs. During the summer the crane's body and neck feathers are stained a rusty brown from being in the marshes. In early summer, cranes are seen in small flocks and pairs in meadows and marshy areas. They are here to mate and nest. They feed in open meadows and wetlands. Cranes are found in Willow Flats near Jackson Lake Dam, the Snake River bottomlands, and Oxbow Bend.

FUN FACT: Sandhill cranes are one of the oldest bird species on Earth, and their deep, trumpeting call sounds almost prehistoric.

Bald Eagle

This is our national bird. Bald Eagles eat mostly fish but sometimes catch ducks or other animals. An eagle will catch fish in shallow water by swooping down and grabbing them with its sharp talons. If a Bald Eagle sees an Osprey (fish hawk) with a fish it will try to make the Osprey drop it. Watch for them along the Snake River. The Oxbow Bend is a good place to look.

FUN FACT: Bald Eagles are not bald, but have white feathers on their head and tail. These beautiful white feathers don't grow until the eagle is about four years old.

Osprey

The Osprey is sometimes mistaken for an eagle. They have long wings and soar over the water. When the Osprey sees a fish in the water, it dives straight down and hits the water with its feet first. It grabs the fish and then flaps hard to get out of the water. Ospreys nest in a big stick nest on top of dead trees. When their young are grown, the Ospreys fly south for the winter. Oxbow Bend and Jackson Lake Dam are good places to see Ospreys.

FUN FACT: Ospreys have special pads with tiny barbs on the soles of their feet. The barbs help them hold on to slippery fish.

Trumpeter Swan

This is the largest waterfowl (ducks, geese, and swans) in North America. They are huge, graceful white birds with long necks and wide wingspans. Trumpeter Swans are very rare. They nest on islands in small ponds or in big marshes and usually lay one to three eggs. The babies are called cygnets. They are gray when they are small. In winter swans gather on certain streams that don't freeze. The National Elk Refuge usually has Trumpeter Swans on its creeks in winter.

FUN FACT: Trumpeter swans mate for life, and the pairs stay together all through the year.

The Kid's Guide *to* Grand Teton National Park

Raven

The raven is black from head to toe and has a wingspan of four feet. These large birds have long, shaggy throat feathers and long, thick bills. Up close, the feathers can shine with an iridescent purple.

Ravens are great fliers and can be mistaken for hawks at a distance. They have long pointed wings and can be seen soaring, diving, or doing aerobatics. They eat everything from carrion (dead animals) to berries, and they rob eggs from other birds' nests and catch mice.

Ravens are found throughout the park. Many scenic turnouts and picnic areas have ravens hanging out and waiting for careless visitors to leave food behind. Don't do it!

FUN FACT: Raven stories and myths can be found in many cultures. Some people admire the raven's intelligence, but others think these big black birds are signs of trouble.

Sage Grouse

Sage Grouse are large, chicken-like birds with a gray speckled appearance that matches the sagebrush. They have long, pointed tails, white undersides to their wings, and black bellies. During the spring mating season, the male has a black throat and yellow "combs" above its eyes.

These birds are secretive and difficult to see except when they fly up out of the sage. They are also visible during their spectacular spring mating ritual, when the males puff out large white throat sacs, fan their tails, and dance and strut for the hens.

These are strictly sagebrush birds. Look along Antelope Flats Road, as well as along the main highway near the Jackson Hole Airport.

FUN FACT: During the Sage Grouse mating season, park rangers take visitors to watch the grouse dance for each other, but you have to go out at five in the morning!

Raven

GRAY JAY

You will find these playful birds wherever people go. They are attracted to campgrounds and picnic areas. Gray Jays are a little bigger than robins and all gray. They make soft whistle sounds. Gray Jays are also known as "Camp Robbers" because they like to swoop down and steal food from picnic tables. They are very tame and friendly, but they should not be fed or encouraged to take food. They are often seen around Jenny Lake Campground and String Lake Picnic Area.

FUN FACT: Gray Jays live here all year. Like other jays, they will steal shiny things such as pennies or tinfoil from visitors.

YELLOW-HEADED BLACKBIRD

This bird is hard to mistake for anything else. Only the male birds are colored like this, though. The females and young birds are mostly brown. Yellow-headed blackbirds live near swamps and marshes and build their nest in the tall reeds. The female weaves a nest out of grass attached to several reeds so it stays off the wet ground.

FUN FACT: Their call is not a pretty song and sounds more like a squeaky-voiced bird trying to sing.

BLACK-BILLED MAGPIE

This is the only bird that looks like this—black and white with a long, long tail. As it flies, it looks as if it is riding along on big waves—up and down and up. If you see one up close, you will notice that the black feathers are actually "iridescent" and greenish in sunlight. Magpies are scavengers and eat animals that have died or been killed. They also catch insects and other small prey.

FUN FACT: Magpies build a nest in the bushes made out of sticks and shaped like a ball with a hole in one side.

Mountain BLUEBiRD

Male bluebirds are a soft, brilliant blue, and the females are bluish-gray with a gray breast. They are relatively tame birds, robin-like but smaller. Their call is a quiet little note.

You usually see bluebirds perching on fence posts, tall weeds or shrubs, or on signposts around the park. They nest in hollows in aspen and cottonwood trees. They like open meadows along Antelope Flats Road, Moose-Wilson Road, and in Lupine Meadows.

FUN FACT: Mountain Bluebirds flutter gently down from their perches to catch insects on the ground.

Spotted Sandpiper

In spring and summer, when the birds are most numerous here, this small shorebird has distinct spots on its belly as well as its back. Spotted Sandpipers are about six to seven inches long.

The Spotted Sandpiper walks along the shores of streams and lakes, bobbing its tail constantly.

The shores of the Snake River, the mud flats of Oxbow Bend, and just about any small body of water in the park can be home to these birds.

FUN FACT: This sandpiper flies from place to place with a fluttering, rapid wing beat and its wings curved downward.

western Tanager

This medium-sized tanager looks almost like a tropical bird with its yellow body, red face and head, and black back and wings. The female is a duller yellow and has no red on its head.

Western Tanagers arrive in the valley in large, colorful flocks of hundreds of birds. Once they arrive on their nesting territories, they are more secretive and harder to see. Western Tanagers like open forests, especially Lodgepole Pines on moraines. Look for them along the hiking trails not far from the trailheads, around Jenny Lake, and near Signal Mountain.

FUN FACT: Some people who see a colorful Western Tanager for the first time think that a parrot has escaped!

MANY-FLoWeReD PHLoX

Phlox grows close to the ground in a thick "mat" of flowers. There are five white petals, and each flower is about as big as a quarter. There are other phlox plants in the park with blue or purplish flowers.

FUN FACT: Phlox is one of the wildflowers that people grow in their flower gardens.

YaMPaH

You might see Yampah near the trails as you hike in the park. It grows in meadows. Yampah is about one to three feet tall with a bunch of thin branches at the top and lots of little white flowers. Yampah has a root like a fat carrot.

FUN FACT: In the springtime, bears and other animals dig up Yampah roots for food. American Indians used to eat them, too.

CoLoRaDo CoLUMBine

Look along the hiking trails for this very beautiful wildflower. It usually grows in grassy places in the shade of trees. The flowers are on top of tall stalks and have five big petals that sweep back into long spurs. You will find them in July and August along the canyon trails.

FUN FACT: This same flower is blue in the state of Colorado.

SHoWY GReen GenTiaN

You may walk right past this flower and think it is just a tall green stalk or weed, but if you look closely you'll see its delicate little blossoms. The petals are whitish-green with purple spots, and many insects are attracted to their pollen. This plant can be up to five feet tall.

FUN FACT: In the first year, this plant is only a whorl (round shape) of leaves near the ground. In the second year, it grows tall, produces flowers, and dies.

ARROWLEAF BALSAMROOT

In early summer, you will see this flower growing all over the valley and low hills in the park. It grows in a big clump of large, light-green leaves with bright yellow flowers. It gets its name from the leaves, which are shaped like arrowheads.

FUN FACT: Balsamroot is a good food plant and is eaten by elk and deer.

MULES-EAR

Just about the time that the Arrowleaf Balsamroot starts to die another yellow flower takes its place. This is Mules-ear, named for its big leaves that look like the animal's ears.

FUN FACT: Mules-ear is easy to tell from Balsamroot by its shiny, dark green leaves instead of dull, light green ones.

YELLOW MONKEYFLOWER

If you stop to admire one of the little creeks that crosses a trail in the mountains, you might see this flower. It grows right on the bank and often hangs out over the water. The flower looks like a snapdragon flower in your garden.

FUN FACT: American Indians used to eat fresh monkeyflower leaves as lettuce.

GLACIER LILY

These lilies grow in the mountain meadows and in the canyons. Other wild lilies include violets and onions. The flowers face down with the petals curving back. Each plant has just two big leaves at the base of the stem.

FUN FACT: Lilies usually have a fat root called a bulb (like the onion) and are eaten by American Indians as well as bears.

INDIAN PAINTBRUSH

This pretty red flower is the state flower of Wyoming. There are several kinds of paintbrushes in the park, including a yellow one. Paintbrush has a special kind of flower—you don't see the actual petals because they are tiny and covered up with colorful red "bracts" that protect the flower.

FUN FACT: Paintbrush plants have roots that poke into other plants' roots and take food.

FIREWEED

This tall flower gets its name from the fact that it is one of the first plants to show up after a forest fire. The plants grow up to six feet tall. In late summer, the fireweed plant is covered with long, silky tufts that blow away in the wind and carry the flower seeds to new places.

FUN FACT: The flowers blossom from the bottom of the plant up.

SKYROCKET GILIA

Five bright scarlet red petals on each flower and lots of flowers at the top of the plant tell you that this is the Skyrocket Gilia (with a "hard" G like in "geese," Gee'-lee-uh). The flowers are trumpet-shaped.

FUN FACT: Skyrocket Gilia can fill a whole meadow.

STICKY GERANIUM

Geraniums grow in open forests and in the sagebrush. The plants can be two feet tall with lots of blossoms. The rosy-purple flowers have five petals with dark pink lines in them.

FUN FACT: When the seeds get ripe, their case splits open and pops out the seeds.

Silver Lupine

Silver Lupine often fills the meadows with its rich blue and purple flowers. Lupine flowers are not regular shaped and have little wings.

FUN FACT: You are almost sure to see this beautiful flower if you go to Lupine Meadows in the early summer.

Hairy Clematis (Sugarbowl)

This little blue flower grows singly on thin stems. The flower bends over and points to the ground. It is shaped like a sugar bowl. Clematis grows in cool, moist places like forests and canyons.

FUN FACT: The whole plant is covered with thin, silky white hairs.

Showy Fleabane

If you know what a daisy flower looks like, you will be able to tell this one when you see it. The center disc is bright yellow-orange and the petals, called rays, are purple or bluish white.

FUN FACT: Each flower is a little bigger than a quarter, and they grow in bunches.

Harebell

You can find these pretty little flowers growing in the pine and spruce forests. Look around Jenny Lake and along the trails into the mountains. The flowers look like little bells hanging down.

FUN FACT: You might find an all white "albino" harebell sometime.

HANDS ON!

A national park is not like a museum. Even though the land is protected, you can touch things, hike, swim, and experience the natural world that has been set aside for everyone. You just have to be careful not to move anything, take anything, or harm any of the plants or animals.

Programs led by rangers will introduce you to nature and how to be in the outdoors. These group programs are fun and informative even if you are an experienced camper or hiker.

JUNIOR RANGERS PROGRAM

If you participate in the Junior Rangers Program, you will learn what it's like to be a park ranger. Learn why everything in the park needs to be preserved, how to protect the plants and animals, and how to look for wildlife. If you are from eight to twelve years old, you can earn your Junior Rangers badge or your Junior Naturalist patch.

One of the things Junior Rangers might learn about is wildfire. Most of the natural fires caused by lightning are allowed to burn because they help make the forests and meadows healthy. Sometimes rangers start small fires to clear away dead plants and make room for new ones to sprout. If you see smoke, ask a ranger if it is from a wildfire or a "prescribed" fire.

Natural wildfire actually helps the forest.

In the park, you can pick things up if you put them back.

EXPERIENCE THE OUTDOORS

Remember, one of the main reasons this valley is set aside as a national park is so you can see what the land was like before it was changed by people. The only way to do that is to get out of the car and see for yourself, even if it's raining, or windy, or hot and sunny. That's the way nature is. Look at the ground and you will see no green lawns. Look at the trees and you will see that some of them are dead, some are old, and some are young. There are no fences. No one sprays chemicals to kill insects. "Nature" means a place where things happen naturally.

Exploring near a beaver pond.

HIKING

Hiking is the most popular way to get out into the park. Grand Teton National Park has over 200 miles of trails. You can get a trail map at the visitor center and see where you want to go. Some of the trails are easy, and some are difficult. Here are a few suggestions to start.

LEIGH LAKE (Easy) Two to four miles there and back. (two to the lake and back, four to the great view spots)

TAGGART LAKE (Easy) Just over three miles there and back.

HIDDEN FALLS AND CASCADE CANYON (Longer and a bit harder than Taggart Lake) Only one mile to the falls and back if you ride the boat across Jenny Lake.

DEATH CANYON (Somewhat difficult but easy in places) Less than one mile to the overlook to Phelps Lake, then down a steep trail and into Death Canyon. Don't worry about the name—this canyon is beautiful and full of life.

CAMPING

JHHSM BC.103

Early campers, Cliff and Sylvia

Early cookout at a dude ranch

There is nothing quite like camping out in a national park. The air is clear, birds and wildlife are all around you, and you can see the stars at night.

Since so many people want to camp in the park, there are campgrounds set up. These are the only places you can camp. If people camped wherever they wanted to it would disturb the wildlife and harm the plants.

There are two kinds of camping areas. At regular campgrounds your family parks their car nearby, there are restrooms, and there is water. You can often have a campfire at these campgrounds. (See the map at the back of the book.)

The other kind of camping is in the backcountry. You have to have a permit to camp, and you have to hike or canoe to get there. The rangers at the visitor centers can tell you how to get a permit and what you need to take with you.

SWiMMiNG

You can swim in any of the lakes or streams in the park, but there are a few places that are closed for your safety. Most of the streams here are very cold, and many of them are dangerous to swim in. The lakes are usually warmer. They can be deep and cold as well, but there are some beautiful places with perfect swimming.

Swimming in a mountain lake is one of the most refreshing things you can do. The water is clear, there are no chemicals in it, and when you get out you feel great. Here are a few good places to swim:

STRING LAKE

String Lake is between Jenny Lake and Leigh Lake. You turn at the North Jenny Lake Junction and follow the signs to the big parking area. There are picnic tables, restrooms, and, if it's a warm day, you'll see people swimming.

LEIGH LAKE

You hike to Leigh Lake, which makes the swimming even better. Park at the same place as for String Lake and take the trail to Leigh Lake. You will see some small beaches with white sand along the lake shore.

JACKSON LAKE

This is a huge, cold lake, but it gets warm in July and August. Some of the best gravel beaches for swimming are at Signal Mountain and Colter Bay.

DANGERS OF COLD WATER SWIMMING

If you aren't used to cold water, be careful! It can take your breath away and make your muscles get tired quickly. Stay near shore, and swim in water where you can touch the bottom.

Mount Moran reflected in String Lake

Boating

Boating is a great way to see the park away from roads and other people. If your family has a boat or canoe, all you need is a park boat permit and a map. Rangers at the visitor centers can help you decide where to go. Canoes are allowed on all the lakes and the Snake River, but the Snake requires experience in boating on fast rivers.

If you don't have a boat, you can rent canoes and rowboats in the park. The visitor centers have information on boat rentals. You can also pay to ride a boat on Jackson Lake or to ride across Jenny Lake to Hidden Falls. One of the most popular boating rides in GTNP is a raft trip on the Snake River. You can find out about those at the visitor centers, too.

Fishing

Many of the lakes and streams in the park are open for fishing. You need to have a Wyoming fishing license, or your parent needs to have one if you are under fourteen years old. Fishing is also a good way to see wildlife because you are near water and wildlife often visits to drink. It can be especially good wildlife viewing if you fish early in the morning or late in the day.

Remember, these fish are all part of the nature of the park, and if you aren't going to keep them they need to be treated very carefully. Get your hands wet, hold the fish gently, and set them back (don't throw them) into the water.

WHO WAS THE FIRST TO CLIMB THE GRAND TETON?

No one knows for sure because the first person may have been an American Indian or an early explorer who didn't leave any evidence. The first we know for sure was in 1898, when William Owen, John Shive, Franklin Spaulding, and Frank Petersen made it to the top.

WHO WAS THE FASTEST?

On August 12, 2012, a Spanish mountain runner named Kilian Jornet ran from the Lupine Meadows parking lot to the top of the Grand Teton and back down to the parking lot in just two hours and fifty-four minutes!

WHO WAS THE FIRST WOMAN?

Eleanor Davis was the first woman to climb the Grand, and she went up in 1923. The second woman was retired school teacher named Geraldine Lucas. She was fifty-nine.

WHO WAS THE FIRST CLIMBER TO FALL AND DIE?

In 1925, a man named Theodore Teepe was climbing down off the Grand Teton, slid on a glacier and died when he hit some rocks.

Climbers practicing to go up the Grand Teton

CLIMBING

A really good way to see how wonderful the Tetons are is to climb to the top of one. But mountain climbing is very dangerous if you don't know what you are doing. The best way to learn is to go to one of the approved climbing schools in the park. There are two: The Exum Guide Service and Jackson Hole Mountain Guides. There is information about them at the visitor centers.

These two climbing schools can teach you how to climb safely. It takes two or three days to learn the basic climbing moves and how to use ropes and other gear. If you finish the school and learn to climb safely, you can hire a guide to take you up one of the peaks.

It's a long way to the top!

Ouch! Old time climbing boot

Fun Places

Colter Bay Swim Beach

If you like to skip stones or just sit on a lakeshore, you'll like this place. It is right on the shore of Jackson Lake. This is a great spot to swim in the lake—just be sure you test the water for warmth first and stay near shore. The lake can be very cold, and the water is deep. You can fish here for lake trout, too. Watch out for thunderstorms that may come across the lake from the mountains.

String Lake

This is the perfect place for a family picnic. There are lots of picnic tables, and the lake is close by. This is one of the warmest and nicest places to swim in the park. The water is clear and shallow near the shore for good wading. The middle is deeper, and there are big fish. This is also a great spot to canoe, kayak, or float on an air mattress. Storms can come over the mountains quickly, so keep your eyes open for clouds.

Jenny Lake Boat Ride

Even if you like to hike, this is a fun way to get across Jenny Lake to start your hike to Hidden Falls or Inspiration Point. The boat leaves from the dock near the Jenny Lake parking area and goes across to the West Shore near the mountains. You have to pay a fee to ride the boat. Be sure to find out when the last boat of the day comes back so you don't miss it, or you'll have to walk back around the lake.

Colter Bay Indian Arts Museum

If you want to know more about American Indians, this is the place to go. There are beautiful displays of all kinds of Indian arts, clothing, and other items. During certain hours there will be an American Indian at work making jewelry or other fine art. There is also a small bookstore where you can get books about hiking and other activities. The museum is a great place to spend a rainy day.

Jackson Lake Dam

This spot is not exactly a wilderness experience, but you can see and learn a lot here. The dam was built in 1911, to raise the water level in the lake and save irrigation water for farmers during late summer. There was once a town here when the dam was being built. This is a popular place to fish for trout, just downstream. Since there are lots of fish, it is a good place to see Bald Eagles, Ospreys, White Pelicans, and even river otters.

Summit of Signal Mountain

This mountain was named for the night long ago that a signal fire was lit by a search party looking for a man on the river. The fire was to signal other searchers that his body had been found. The road was built to the top when there was a fire lookout here. Signal Mountain is a good place to see the whole Jackson Hole valley, the mountains, and the lakes. You can see how the melting glaciers washed down the valley and left channels and terraces. This is the place to watch a colorful sunset and to see a Blue Grouse on the trail or along the road.

Visitor Centers

The National Park Service has several visitor centers in the park. The largest one is at Moose. These centers are where you get information and permits, look at maps, get help from rangers, or buy books about the park.

GET YOUR BOOK STAMPED FOR FREE AT THE VISITOR CENTERS

Moose

The Craig Thomas Discovery and Visitor Center offers lots of exhibits about the park, its geology and natural history, and about the human history. This is where you can reserve camp sites, get boat permits, and find information about hiking into the backcountry. Moose also has the largest bookstore in the park, and you can find information on just about anything here.

Jenny Lake

This small visitor center is in an old log cabin that once belonged to a photographer. His name was Harrison Crandall, and he built this cabin by hand. This visitor center has some of everything in it—a few exhibits, a few books, and lots of information. Jenny Lake is the area where mountain climbers register to go into the peaks. Across the creek is the mountain climbing school.

Jenny Lake Visitor Center when it was an art studio

Jenny Lake Visitor Center today

Heron Pond near Colter Bay

COLTER BAY

Located right on the shore of Jackson Lake, Colter Bay is a village in itself. At the visitor center you can get permits for camping and boating, buy guidebooks and ask questions. There are shops, places to eat, cabins, a campground, and a marina where you can rent a boat. The visitor center shows park videos throughout the day. This is also where the Indian Arts Museum is located.

FLAGG RANCH

This visitor center is in the north end of the valley and is actually outside of the park. It is in the John D. Rockefeller, Jr. Memorial Parkway. This is a strip of land between Grand Teton and Yellowstone parks, so there is information on both places. Like all the other visitor centers, you can get ideas on what to see and where to go.

©2006 Grand Teton Association

Grand Teton National Park

P.O. Box 170, Moose WY 83012

www.grandtetonpark.org

Series Design by

Jeff Pollard Design & Associates

Maps by

Mike Reagan

Project Coordinated by

Jan Lynch, Executive Director,

Grand Teton Association

Printed by

Paragon Press

ISBN 978-0-931895-66-1